Suite from
WEST SIDE STORY®

for Violin and Piano

Based on a conception by Jerome Robbins

Book by
Arthur Laurents

Music by
Leonard Bernstein®

Lyrics by
Stephen Sondheim

Entire original production
directed and choreographed by
Jerome Robbins

Concert Arrangement for violin and piano by
Raimundo Penaforte

CONTENTS

ISBN 978-1-4234-1148-2

LEONARD
BERNSTEIN
Music Publishing
Company LLC

BOOSEY &HAWKES

HAL•LEONARD®
CORPORATION
7777 W. BLUEMOUND RD. P.O. BOX 13819 MILWAUKEE, WI 53213

Visit Hal Leonard Online at **www.halleonard.com**

This suite from *West Side Story*® was recorded by violinist Chee-Yun and pianist Akira Eguchi on the Denon Records release, *Vocalise* (Denon CO-75118).

I Feel Pretty	3:15
Somewhere	3:41
America	4:20

I FEEL PRETTY

from "West Side Story"

for violin and piano

Leonard Bernstein

Arranged by Raimundo Penaforte

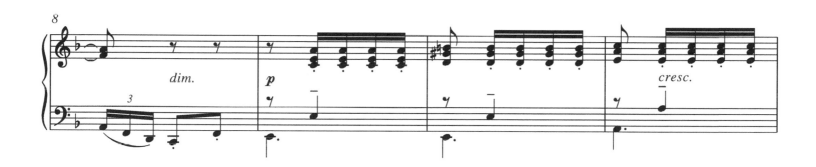

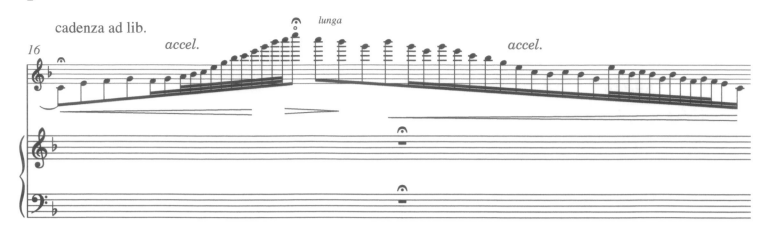

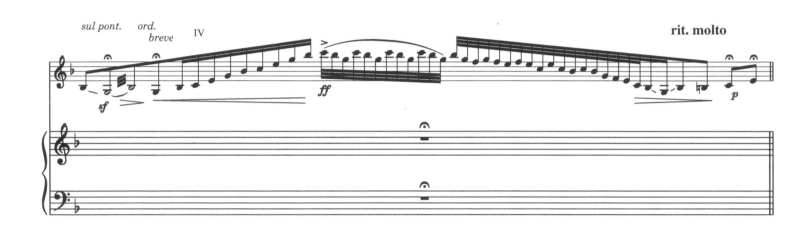

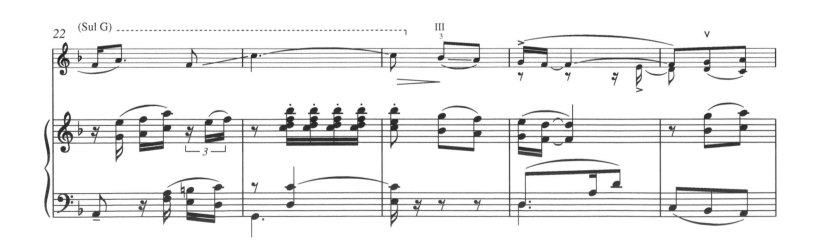

attacca

SOMEWHERE

from "West Side Story"

Leonard Bernstein
Arranged by Raimundo Penaforte

AMERICA
from "West Side Story"

Leonard Bernstein
Arranged by Raimundo Penaforte